Intermediate
Spanish
Memory
Book

Intermediate Spanish Memory Book

A New Approach to Vocabulary Building

William F. Harrison and
Dorothy Winters Welker

 University of Texas Press
Austin

Copyright © 1997 by the University of Texas Press

Requests for permission to reproduce material from this work should be sent to Permissions, University of Texas Press, P.O. Box 7819, Austin, TX 78713-7819.

Printed in the United States of America

∞ The paper used in this publication meets the minimum requirements of American National Standard for Information Sciences—Permanence of Paper for Printed Library Materials, ANSI Z39.48-1984.

First edition, 1997

Library of Congress Cataloging-in-Publication Data

Harrison, William F., 1934–
    Intermediate Spanish memory book : a new approach to vocabulary building / by William F. Harrison and Dorothy Winters Welker. — 1st ed.
        p.   cm.
    Continues: Spanish memory book.
    ISBN 0-292-73110-8 (alk. paper). —
    ISBN 0-292-73111-6 (pbk. : alk. paper)
    1. Spanish language—Vocabulary.   I. Welker, Dorothy Winters, 1905–   . II. Title.
    PC4445.H37   1997
    468.2'421—dc20   96-31441

CONTENTS

TO THE READER

The book in your hands is the sequel to the *Spanish Memory Book*. The main difference between that book and the *Intermediate Spanish Memory Book* is that the vocabulary of this book is slightly more advanced than that of the first *Spanish Memory Book*. You can begin with either book and then pass to the other without difficulty.

As with the first *Spanish Memory Book,* your goal will be to increase your store of Spanish words. When you have completed both books you will have a vocabulary of some 1,250 useful words for speaking, reading, and writing Spanish. All of the *Spanish Memory Books* are designed to help you learn Spanish words easily and rapidly and to recall them at will. They will enable you to recognize Spanish words when you see or hear them (passive vocabulary), and to recall these words when you speak or write Spanish (active vocabulary).

As in the first *Spanish Memory Book,* this is accomplished by means of mnemonic devices (memory helps). Mnemonic devices are not new, of course; they have been used for centuries. We still call upon them every day to remember names, numbers, and many other things. In the *Memory Books,* each mnemonic device sets up an association between a new word and one or more familiar words that enables us to recall the new word. The mnemonic devices used in these books are rhymes that help you to remember both the pronunciation of the Spanish words and their English meanings. They fairly jingle the new words into your memory.

Research has shown that the more far-fetched, even absurd, a mnemonic device is, the better it helps you remember. You will probably agree that many of the jingles in the *Spanish Memory Books* qualify for high marks in absurdity! You will have a good time learning and applying them.

HOW TO USE THE
Intermediate Spanish Memory Book

Each jingle in this book gives you two pieces of information about a Spanish word: 1) its sound (pronunciation), including stress (accent), and 2) its sense (meaning). The jingle helps you store in your memory both the sound and the sense of the word. In each jingle the stress falls on the stressed syllable of the Spanish word. The jingle also contains the English equivalent of the key word. You need not memorize any lyric in its entirety; just remember the significant parts.

The following jingle will show you how the method works.

presión (f.)   pressure

Pray see only the wealth of good in Gerty.
Sure it's the **pressure** of poverty makes her dirty.

The Spanish word to be learned is presión, English "pressure." Incorporated in the jingle is a series of words or parts of words that reproduce the sounds of Spanish presión. These words are **Pray see** plus **on** of **on**ly. These words, which are underscored, are always consecutive; you don't have to search for them through a maze of unrelated sounds. Read the underscored syllables aloud carefully, making sure you pronounce them exactly as you do in the English word. You have just pronounced Spanish "presión." Then note the corresponding English word "pressure," which is also incorporated in the jingle and is in bold print.

Now look away from the book and ask yourself, What is the Spanish word for "pressure"? Chances are you will come up promptly with presión. If not, just read the jingle once more.

Here is another example.

cebada   barley

We all **say** "**Bah! The** charge is false that Charlie
Has planted marijuana with the **barley**."

Here, **say Bah! The** repeats the sounds of Spanish cebada. The
English equivalent is "barley."
     And here is one more. Do it on your own.

puño   fist

The s**poon Yo**landa thrust into my trembling **fist**
Was full of pills provided by the court psychologist.

CONVENTIONS USED IN THIS BOOK

1. As far as possible, the jingles reproduce the exact sounds of the Spanish words. When exactitude is not possible, the Spanish sounds are approximated. For the fine points of pronunciation, turn to a Spanish textbook or to your Spanish teacher. A pronunciation guide is provided in this book as a convenient reference.

2. Two consonants, r and rr, need special treatment. See the Pronunciation Guide in this book.

3. Spanish single vowel sounds are always tense as contrasted with English vowel sounds, which may end in a semi-vowel.

4. The main Spanish entry always gives the infinitive of verbs and the singular of nouns. The pronunciation demonstrated in the jingle applies to these basic forms. In the jingles the English equivalent of the Spanish entry may appear in any convenient form. For example, a verb may be in any tense, and a noun may be either singular or plural.

5. The gender of nouns is given except for nouns ending in o, which are usually masculine, or in a, usually feminine. Endings are given for nouns and adjectives that have a masculine form ending in o and a feminine form ending in a.

6. This book conforms with the latest rules for alphabetizing Spanish words established by the Royal Academy of the Spanish Language in 1994. Ch is no longer considered a separate letter,

but is two letters: c and h. Similarly, ll is now treated as two separate letters: l and l. In short, there are no significant differences in alphabetizing between Spanish and English.

Note: The *Memory Books* are aimed primarily at helping you learn vocabulary. They cannot give conjugations of verbs or rules of sentence structure, which are the concern of grammar. To do so would reduce the number of words that could be included and would encroach on the territory of language teachers and of grammar textbooks.

PRONUNCIATION GUIDE

This section is included to serve as a reference in case you wish to refresh your memory of the basic rules of Spanish pronunciation.

VOWELS AND DIPHTHONGS

Spanish	*English Approximation*
a	a in father
ai /ay /all	aye
au	town
e	take
ei /ey	weigh; similar to Spanish e, but longer
i	machine
io /yo	yoke
o	no
oi /oy /oll	boy
u	Susan; silent between g and i, between g and e, and after q
ua	squat
ue	way
ui /uy /ull	we
uo	woe
b/v	banana at the beginning of a sentence or of a word-group within a sentence and after m or n; elsewhere the lips barely meet
c	cat before a, o, u, or a consonant; sat before i or e

Spanish	*English Approximation*
ch	chart
d	dog at the beginning of a sentence or of a word-group within the sentence, and following n or l; elsewhere d approximates the th in they
f	fin
g	go before a, o, u; strongly aspirated h before i and e
h	always silent
j	strongly aspirated h
l	little
ll	yes
m	mother
n	like English n except preceding m, b, f, and v, when it is pronounced m
ñ	canyon
p	spy
q	q is always followed by silent u; the combination is pronounced like k in kite
r	after n, l, and s and at the beginning of a word r is trilled; the resulting sound is something like the one children produce in imitating a motor; elsewhere r approximates the tt in potty
rr	always trilled
s	so; s before d and g is pronounced like z in zebra
t	task
x	socks; in a few Indian words such as México and Oaxaca x is pronounced like a strongly aspirated h
y	y in yes; when y stands alone it approximates the e in equal
z	so

Intermediate
Spanish
Memory
Book

VOCABULARY

abanico   fan

Says **B<u>ob on eco</u>**logical decay:
"No **fan** can blow the smell of death away!"

abono   fertilizer

I, **B<u>ob, owe no</u>** man for food or **fertilizer**,
And you could say the same if you were somewhat wiser!

abrigar   to cherish, harbor, shelter

—**B<u>ob, regar</u>**d the market news; it's bearish!
—Ah, your opinion's not the one I **cherish**!

abril   April

On **April** Fool's, though teasing badly,
B<u>ob real</u>ly showed he loves you madly.

aburrido, -a   bored, boring

<u>Ah, boor, wreathe o</u>ld pipes with smoke;
And don't get **bored** with one small joke!

aburrir   to bore

<u>Abou, rear</u> that girl in distant places,
So she won't **bore** us making silly faces.

achacar   to impute, put the blame on

The choppy ch**a–cha Car**la no doubt dances well,
But don't **impute** to that wild girl the graces of a belle!

acometer (1)   to attack

P**a, Coe may tear** us limb from limb!
If he **attacks**, look out for him!

acometer (2)   to undertake

Ah, Coe, may terrorists no more pursue you,
Or **undertake** a struggle to undo you!

acrecentar   to increase

Ach! Ray sent Arthur orders **to increase**
Looting and burning in the cause of peace.

actriz   actress

The boss d**ocked Reese**'s pay because
Of all the **actresses** he paws!

actuar   to actuate, activate

Ach! too ardent is your kiss!
It takes a gentler love than this
To actuate a lover's bliss.

afeitar   to shave

P**a, Fay tar**nished her repute
By **shaving** costs and hiding loot.

aferrar   to hold, grip, anchor

Ah, fair Arbie, **hold** me close,
At least until I'm comatose!

agobiar   to overwhelm, weigh down

Ah, Gobi, are your tropic sands so hot
A caravan **o'erwhelmed** is left to rot?

agosto   August

Ah, ghost, omit your customary groans.
This **August** day's too hot for rattling bones!

ahorro   thrift, savings

Ah, oar, row swiftly, strongly, and in the name of **thrift**.
We'll row across the lake to save the postage on our gift.

aislar   to insulate, isolate

Ice largely forms Augustus' summer diet.
This **insulates** him—keeps him cool and quiet.

álamo   poplar, cottonwood

M**oll, a mo**torist, speeds blindly by
A row of **poplars** reaching for the sky.
So, speeding but unheeding, there go I.

alarde (m.)   display, ostentation

Say, M**oll, are they** really mere **display**—
The cars, the clothes, the cash you give away?

alegar   to dispute, argue

M**a, lay gar**ments out—and don't **dispute**
This is the time to wear my Sunday suit.

alfombra   rug, carpet

The girl in an **all-foam bra**ssiere was clad,
In which she cut a **rug** that drove men mad!

alguien   someone, somebody

D**oll, ghee en**tering the U.S.A.
Someone clearly has to wrap and weigh.

allá   there, far away

B**uy yo**nder sacred books and read. I swear
Your pious looks alone won't get you **there**!

almohada   pillow

Almo (ah, the "rogue"!) was wont to say,
"Share my **pillow** now or go away!"

alojar   to lodge

Ah, low harp arpeggios fill the air,
Lodge in my breast, and store their sweetness there.

alumno   student

See the sierr**a loom: no** beast, no bird.
We **students** find this nature trip absurd.

amarrar   to moor, tie

Did Pa and M**a mar Ar**thur's dreams
Of **mooring** boats on tropic streams?

ambiente (m.)   atmosphere, environment

D**ombey ente**rtains his friends, I hear,
With talk of dangers in the **atmosphere**!

amparo   refuge, protection, shelter

The great sw**amp Pa wro**te learned books about
Is now a **refuge** for a school of trout.

amplio, -a   wide, ample

Though Tom spoke forcefully at our convention,
The c**alm plea O**wen made got **wide** attention.

anca   rump, buttock (of an animal)

D**on, ca**pitulate! Your wife's a grump!
Give her a friendly pat upon the **rump**!

anhelo   longing

Impatient Sar**a, nail o**ld boards together,
And soothe your **longing** for some sailing weather
By building model boats amid the heather.

anoche   last night

Ah! No chaste maiden would think right
The things you said to me **last night**.

ansiar   to long for

Phr**onsie, ar**gue as you will:
Joe **longs for** you, you long for Bill.

ante   before (place)

D**on, ta**ke up a civic task—some zestful occupation
Like beating up a thug **before** the now indignant nation.

antes (de)   before (time)

D**on, tas**te Ella's skill in ballroom dancing
Before you try your own in rough romancing!

antojo   whim

Impelled by some obscure, heroic **whim**,
We clung **on toe-ho**lds to the crater's rim.

anual   annual

Now comes the **annual** election hour,
And **ah! new ol**igarchs will be in power!

aplacar   to calm, placate

Pop, Loch Arden lies beyond the town.
We'll get there yet if I can **calm** you down.

aplastar   to crush, flatten

Pop lost Arlie when he chanced **to crush**
Her nosegay in the subway's nightly rush.

apoderar(se)   to seize, take possession of

Ah, Poe, there are Satanic implications
In talk of **seizing** the United Nations!

apreciar   to appreciate

Ah, pray C.R. appreciates
The pains you take to keep your dates!

aprobar   to approve, approve of

Ah, probe Arthur's love affairs so numerous!
Do we **approve** because we find them humorous?

apuesto, -a   handsome, elegant

You, **Pop, waste o**r damage **handsome** jewels
By cutting them with simple garden tools.

arar   to plow

Are arguments a means of settling questions
Or just a way **to plow** up indigestions?

arena   sand

A rain arrived and soaked our little band.
All night we shivered in the cold, wet **sand**.
(Of course we told the boss, "Your fete was grand!")

arquitecto   architect

Sure, **Arky, take to**bacco. (I assume
You've had an **architect** design your tomb!)

arrollar   to overwhelm, run over

P**a, Roy ar**dently began the game,
But our boys **overwhelmed** him just the same.

arroz (m.)   rice

A roast with **rice**, done in a trice,
Would last for days if it weren't for mice.

arte (m. and f.)   art

The st**ar te**quila-makers in our shop
Will use their **art** to satisfy your pop.

asalto   assault

Basalt or flint without a flaw or fault
Will give us arrows for our last **assault**.

astro   star

The ancient **Ostro**goths were sons of Mars.
They used to read the future in the **stars**.

atajar   to restrain; intercept

—**Mata Har**i captivates the nation.
To lie, to spy, to die is her vocation.
—**Restrain** the girl—or put her on probation!

atentar   to attempt (as a crime)

Pa, ten Tartars came here **to attempt**
To look for bonds completely tax-exempt.

atrasar   to set back (clock), retard

"**D**ot," **Ross ar**gued, "Now we're in the prisoner's dock.
This time, let's tell the truth. We can't **set back** the clock."

aún   yet, even, still

Pa, Oona's her outlandish name,
And **yet** I love her just the same.

aventajar   to excel, surpass

Pa bent a Harvard ear to those **excelling**
So stoutly in the genteel art of yelling.

ayuda   help, aid

Aye! you, the prettiest of our crowd,
When I with sudden pain was bowed
Refused your **help** and laughed out loud.

ayudar   to help, assist

Hi, you thar behind the billboard lurking,
Why don't you **help**? How come you guys aren't working?

azar (m.)   evil chance, hazard

Ah, Sergeant, 'twas an **evil chance**
That you invited me to dance.

azotar   to lash, whip

Ah, so tardily I came
They **lashed** me with the whip of shame.

baile (m.)   dance (n.)

Let's **buy la**te-closing yellow daffodils,
And watch their **dance** upon our window-sills,
Then scatter to the winds our unpaid bills!

bandera   flag, banner

How could a Bour**bon dare a** Hapsburg to revile?
Let each salute the other's **flag** and share a wary smile.

barbería   barbershop

Please **bar Berea** from my **barbershop**.
My ancient shears just cannot cut her mop.

barrera   barrier, fence

We'll not **bar e'er a** refugee
Who leaped a **barrier** to be free.

¡basta!   enough!

Bah! statistics show that life is tough.
Another day, and I'll just cry, "**Enough**!"

bélico, -a   warlike, martial

The **bay Lee co**mbed each day for deep-sea treasures
Is now the site of all our **warlike** measures.

billete (m.)   ticket (in Spain), bank note

Yeay, **Bee, yeay! ta**ke out a **ticket**.
You can't resist a game of cricket!

bocado   bite, mouthful

This dra**b oak, ah! though** stung by blight,
Still yields my horse a leafy **bite**.

bodega   storeroom; corner store; wine cellar

Bo**bo, they go**t more and MORE room
By just converting that old **storeroom**.

bola   ball, sphere

Our silver **ball** and golden **bowl a**ppealed to every guest,
Especially the one who hid them underneath his vest.

boleto   ticket

Bo, let Tobias use your **ticket**.
For after all, it's only cricket!

bolsa   purse

The day I found a **bowl Sa**lome painted,
I sighed, I put it in my **purse**—and fainted.

bono (1)   bond, voucher

Your **beau, no** doubt, holds **bonds** and stocks,
So why's he always on the rocks?

bono (2)   bonus

A **bone o**'erlooked by that wild band
To Fido seemed a **bonus** grand.

bostezo   yawn (n.)

You, **Bo, stay so** doggedly till dawn
That conversation fades into a **yawn**.

brasa   red-hot coal

The **bra Sa**mantha so extols
Inflames my sense like **red-hot coals**.

brea   sackcloth; tar

Oh, **bray a** bit more softly, gentle ass,
And let the penitents in **sackcloth** pass.

brillo   luster, shine

The **Brie Yo**landa lightly spread
Gave life and **luster** to her bread,
But Roger asked for ham instead.

brindar   to drink a toast

Find a ca**b, 'Reen dar**ling, then out to **drink a toast**
To all the boys and girls out there we love and hate the most!

brío   brio, enthusiastic vigor

—De**bris, o**ld top, chokes up my mental drains.
—Come, sweep them out with **brio**, brawn, and brains!

bulla   noise, bustle, clatter

The "**Boo" ya** heard burst forth from little Kitty,
Half maddened by the **noises** of the city.

bulto   bundle

Arriving with his **bundle** in fabled Istan**bul**,
Tobias knew no Arabic, but tried to keep his cool.

cabo   end

Corn on the **cob—o**ld-fashioned dish—
Meets in the **end** my every wish.

cada   each

Dic**k, ah! the** creatures—**each** can call them what he wishes—
Though served in Haviland or Spode are yet a mess of fishes.

cadena   chain

Dor**ca, they kno**cked out the thief.
Now he's in **chains**, so what's your beef?

cáliz (m.)   chalice, cup, vase

My **collie s**prang, and broke the **chalice**
Some sultan gave to Sister Alice.

cambio   change, shift

—Be **calm, Bee. —O**h, I fear I've lost my shirt!
—In Tuesday's market **change** we've all been hurt.

camisa   shirt

We named our recent sit-**com "Aeso**p's Fables."
But keep you **shirt** on till a network cables.

campana   bell

Calm Pa. Natasha's more than just a name.
It rings a **bell** that tells my father's shame.

canas   gray hair

The **Khan as**serted with an angry glare,
"My harem will not tolerate **gray hair**!"

cántaro   pitcher, jug

Is **Kant a ro**mantic? Oh, no! he's a **pitcher**
Pouring out wine ever sweeter and richer.

carecer   to be in need of, lack

The **car Ace air**s is much **in need of**
Those air brakes we so often read of.

carga   load, burden

His **car ga**lumphed along the road
Till he could dump his grisly **load**.

casar(se)   to marry, wed

—Is Lu**cas sor**ry that he **married** Sue?
—Oh, no. He loves her money. Wouldn't you?

cavar   to excavate, dig

The In**ca bar**red the fort's old oaken door
And then bent down **to excavate** the floor.
He found a pile of bones and nothing more.

cazar   to hunt

The In**ca ser**geant with a grunt
Declared he'd rather fight than **hunt**.

cebada   barley

We all **say "Bah! The** charge is false that Charlie
Has planted marijuana with the **barley**."

ceja   eyebrow

We **say "Ha**noi" mostly with **eyebrows** raised,
Because of news ambiguously phrased.

celoso, -a   jealous, suspicious

Sail oh! so secretly with some new girl!
Somewhere you'll bump into your **jealous** Pearl.

cenar   to dine, have supper

Some **say nar**ks refuse **to dine**
Until they've tasted all the wine.

cercar to fence in, besiege, encircle

Fenced in by want, the farmers have hard sledding.
While toff**s air car**s, we peasants air the bedding.

cerveza beer

Cor**sair, base a** schooner here.
We'll fill its hold with buns and **beer**.

cesar to cease, stop

I don't **say sor**ry crooks—such bums as I and you—
Should **cease** to live. But isn't that the decent thing to do?

charlar to chatter, chat

The mayor had the cops **char lar**ks
That **chattered** in the public parks.

cifrar to abridge, cipher

My friend, **see Fra R**oberto. He's a lifer.
He spends his free time learning how to **cipher**.

cintura waistline, waist

Have you **seen two ra**bbinical guys
With **waistlines** double the largest size?

clavar to nail

Te**cla bar**red me from our nuptial bed.
I wish she'd **nailed** me to a cross instead!

cochero carriage driver

The young **co–chair o**pined our **driver**
Would take us home for just a fiver.

código   code

Coe, the Golden Rule is not a joke:
Rather, a **code** of conduct for the folk.

coger   to catch, collect, seize (In America this
word is sometimes considered obscene.)

Mar**co her**alded the coming of the spring
By **catching** birds and bugs and all that sort of thing.

col (f.)   cabbage

The **cabbage** is **col**d: you can see why I scold you.
Nor can you deny that I've told you and told you!

colmar   to fulfill, fill to the brim, overwhelm

The public finds **coal mar**velous for heating,
But cole slaw best **fulfills** my dreams of eating!

colono   colonist

Ni**ck, O lone o**ld British **colonist**,
Your world is gone, you simply don't exist!

cometa (f.)   kite

We'll ma**ke, O mate, a** lighted paper **kite**
To hurtle like a comet through the night!

cometa (m.)   comet

We'll ma**ke, O mate, a** lighted paper kite
To hurtle like a **comet** through the night!

comprobar   to check, verify

With brush and **comb probe Ar**thur's fuzzy head,
And **check** his tale of bedbugs in his bed!

confirmar   to confirm

Does **Cohn fear mar**tyrdom? I can **confirm**
He slithers out of danger like a worm.

congoja   anguish, grief

I made **Cohn go ho**ck everything we owned.
I shared his **anguish**, so we both got stoned!

conocer   to meet (for the first time), be
                        acquainted with

Coe, no ceremony is required
To meet the topless dancer Freddy hired.

conseguir   to obtain, achieve

Cohn, say ghee requires experience in cooking.
Obtain by stealth a Chinese wok when Cho San isn't looking.

constar (1)   to consist

I've seen **Cohn star** in dramas that **consist** of sober scenes
In which you can't be certain what the author really means.

constar (2)   to be clear, be evident

Cohn stars, it**'s clear**, at every function,
Spreading his lies without compunction.

construir   to build

Cohn, strew eerie glances 'round the room,
And **build** an atmosphere of gloom and doom.

contratar   to hire, engage

Cohn, trot Artemisia from her stall.
I'd like **to hire** her for the jockeys' ball.

convite (m.)   banquet, dinner party

Cohn, beat a path to Margot's door,
But shun her **banquets**—they're a bore.

coro   chorus, choir

—I'd like to **co-ro**mance your lovely lady.
—She's from a **chorus** some consider shady.

corto, -a   short

Relentlessly I'll hound you into **court**,
Old man, and there you'll find your life is **short**.

crimen (m.)   crime

The **Cree, men** say, committed many **crimes**—
Like us, the victims of their life and times.

crujir   to rustle, crack, crackle, creak

The whole **crew hear**s the fabrics **rustle**
When Lady Jane puts on her bustle.

cuerno   horn

Pray, Jac**k, wear no** antique hunting **horn**.
Those things went out of style ere you were born.

cuervo   raven, crow

You and your s**quare bow** tie have come to be a bore.
So, like the **raven**, I am croaking, "Nevermore!"

culebra   snake

S**chool Abra**ham in how to care for **snakes**,
So they can greet him mornings when he wakes.

dañar   to spoil, damage, hurt

—As obstinate King Lear, **don yar**ds of phony ermine.
—I fear you'll **spoil** the tragedy: you treat the cast like vermin!

deber (1)   ought to

One **day bear**s traversed this splendid wild.
Some say we **ought to** leave it undefiled!

deber (2)   to owe

You will, I fancy, some **day bur**y all your many grudges.
Your gold? You'll find you **owe** it to the lawyers and the judges.

delante (de)   in front (of), before (place)

Fri**day Lon ta**kes off at half-past seven
To sober up and kneel **in front** of Heaven.

(en) demasía   excess

To**day, Ma, see a** kitchen in a mess.
When Judy cooks, she does it to **excess**.

demasiado   too, too much

Dame Ossie—ah, though bright and neat—
Does seem to me a bit **too** sweet.

dentro (de)   within

The **dent ro**mance impressed **within** our hearts
Will last until the social season starts.

derecho, -a   right-hand, right (direction)

Sun**day, Ray cho**ked up on hearing
Left- and **right-hand** voters cheering.

derribar   to demolish, overthrow

—You favor milky drinks, so why **demolish dairy bar**s?
—They clutter up the road and set a trap for passing cars.

desayuno   breakfast

In O**dessa, you know** what?
Breakfast's free, all nice and hot!

desbaratar   to destroy, disturb, upset

Des, bar a Tartar from your marriage bed.
He will **destroy** you. Wed some wimp instead!

desde   from

Des, they know I dream of your embrace.
They say I follow you **from** place to place.
And shall I shrink from sharing your disgrace?

desmentir   to belie, disprove

Des meant ears to hear her shrill tirade.
Her gentle looks **belie** the scene she made.

despegar   to loose, detach

Des, pay Garfield what he says we owe.
Tell him to **loose** our chains and let us go!

despejar   to clear, remove obstacles from

—**Des, pay Har**ley good hard cash
To **clear** the ground of last night's trash.
—Oh, what a mess! —But what a bash!

desplegar   to unfold, unfurl

Des, play gardener: at six years old
Your hands can help the crocuses **unfold**.

despreciar   to scorn, despise

Des, pray see art as something we must cherish.
When art **is scorned**, mankind must surely perish.

desviar   to divert, deflect

Des, be artful. When romance
Approaches, don't **divert** your glance!

dibujo   etching, drawing

Dee, boo José. He saw my **etching**.
He says it makes him feel like retching!

diestro, -a   skillful

Have rea**dy estro**gens, in which you're **skillful**,
To help persuade the outlaw if he's willful.

diosa   goddess

An**dy, oh, su**ppose a **goddess** comes
While I am entertaining all these bums!

disgusto   annoyance, displeasure

Cackling, Do**dy's goose to**ld our **annoyance**
At our unwelcome visitor's flamboyance.

doler   to pain

—It **pains** me that I must **dole Er**ic's wages out.
—You might add on a dime if that old bum should pout!

donaire (m.)   wit, elegance

Ricar**do nigh, Ray** tried to show his **wit**,
But no one here could make much sense of it.

dorar   to gild

To speak with can**dor, Ar**thur tends to **gild**
His stories of the savage beasts he's killed.

dosel (m.)   canopy, dais

Fred**do, sell** these **canopies** to kings
To shield their thrones from civil shocks and stings
And help them keep their minds on higher things.

dotar   to provide, endow

My con**do tar**dily decided
A Sunday brunch **should be provided**.

dote (m. and f.)   dower, dowry; natural gift

Kneading **dough ta**kes more than half an hour.
Pa should have bought a mixer for my **dower**.

dueño   landlord, owner

I've never hear**d Wayne yo**del better than this!
Even his **landlord** has blown him a kiss!

dulce   sweet

They'll find a **duel, say** Tom and Jerry,
For both love **sweet** old Typhoid Mary!

empapar   to soak, saturate

L**em, pop Ar**thur into the sink.
Soak him until he has lost his stink.

empleado   clerk, employee

When Jim heard **Em play, ah! though** weary,
He knew a **clerk's** life can be cheery.

empresa (1)   firm (n.)

I heard **Em pray So**l's **firm** would fail,
And all his cronies go to jail.

empresa (2)   undertaking

L**em, pray Sa**brina's done her vaunted baking.
We'll see if she's a cook, or merely faking
This truly formidable **undertaking**.

enano   dwarf

Here **a non-o**bedient **dwarf**
Just knocked his boss right off the wharf!

encorvar   to bend, curve

B**en, core bar**bèd pineapple for supper,
Then **bend** your hands around this picker-upper.

encuentro   meeting

Wh**en Quent ro**manced with your big sister,
At every **meeting**, first he kissed 'er.

enfriar   to cool

Cl**em, free Ar**t from his senseless passion!
Cool his love in your own firm fashion.

engaño   trick, deceit

B**en gone, Yo**landa played a dirty **trick**:
She mixed exotic drinks that made us sick.

enmudecer   to be still, become silent

Just hear th**em! "Moo!" they say, "R**emember—
We'll all **be still** by next December!"

enredo   tangle, entanglement

M**en, Ray, though** caught in a mental **tangle**,
Has learned to think from a different angle.

ensalada   salad

Th**en, Sol (ah! the** woman's cheek is pallid!),
We'll fill her up with guacamole **salad**!

ensayar   to rehearse, practice

Ag**ain, Cy ar**med himself with gin—and worse—
Before he met the players to **rehearse**!

entraña   core, center, entrails

In YOUR t**ent, Ron, ya** reckless hellion,
They found the **core** of the rebellion!

entregar   to deliver, hand over

B**en, Tray gar**nered heaps of bones,
Delivered them to still my groans!

envidia   envy, jealousy

Cl**em, be the a**rtist you were born to be,
And feel no **envy**: art is rich and free.

equipaje (m.)   luggage

We burned your **luggage**. Here's the nitty gritty:
It m**ay keep ah! hay** fever from the city!

equipo   team

If th**ey keep o**ld Tom on the football **team**
All the alumni are bound to scream!

erguir   to erect, set up straight

Ere gear can be assembled for our sports
We must **erect** a viewing-stand of sorts.

esbelto, –a   svelte, lithe

Y**es, belt o**ld Tom and make him groan and writhe.
Remind him he's no longer **svelte** and **lithe**.

escalera   stair, ladder

B**ess, call Ero**s from the realms above
To guide you up the cloudy **stairs** of love.

escena   scene

T**ess, sane a**pproaches to your business troubles
Will let you blow them off the **scene** like bubbles!

esconder   to hide, conceal

Y**es, Cohn, dare** to throw your weight around.
Just **hide** your fears and learn to hold your ground!

escultura   sculpture

B**ess' school tour a**round the city
Taught her **sculpture** can be pretty.

eslabón (m.)   link, bond, tie

Y**es, slob, own** you're nothing but a **link**
Between the garbage and the kitchen sink!

esmero meticulousness

T**ess, may ro**mance forever bloom for you.
Your mate's **meticulousness** will see you through.

espacio space

—**Jess' posse o**nly now has brought the culprit in.
—We have no **space** in jail. So put him in the looney-bin.

esparcir to scatter, spread

Too much neglect and y**es, sparse ir**rigation
May **scatter** ruin on our loved plantation.

esquina corner (street)

—You seem l**ess keen a**bout that crowded **corner**.
—I've found a spot inside, with young Jack Horner.

estera doormat

L**es, tear a** page or two from Mama's journal.
It shows her playing **doormat** to the Colonel.

estirpe (f.) stock, lineage

B**ess, steer Pe**lé away from golf and soccer.
He comes from **stock** that much prefers a rocker.

estupendo, -a stupendous

I gu**ess Stu penned o**ld Silas in the barn,
And made him sit through some **stupendous** yarn.

estúpido, -a stupid

Y**es, Tupi, though** it seems a **stupid** tongue,
Can nonetheless be written, spoken, sung.

evitar   to shun, avoid

Abe, eat Arthur's cheesecake up,
But **shun** the fellow's dirty cup.

examen (m.)   test, examination

Beck's ominous grade on the botany **test**
Proved that his learning was only a jest.

excepto   except

I like the objects of her whims
Except old loves, **except** old hymns.

extraer   to extract, pull out

Some **extra air** has seeped into the vat.
Extract it, or the beer will come out flat.

extrañar   to exile, miss

First, she shall **be exiled** from this place.
N**ext, Ron, yar**ds of costly silk and lace
Shall thinly veil the marks of her disgrace.

extremo   end, extreme

Beck's tray most probably is ready.
Just grab one **end** and hold it steady.

falda   skirt

Yes, Parsi**fal, da**guerrotypes were dim,
But then, they made those long, thick **skirts** look slim.

fardo   bundle, bale

Far though free there lies a blessed land.
So I'll take off, my **bundle** in my hand.

feria   fair (n.)

A **fay, rea**ssessing her magical powers,
Flew to the **fair** in a matter of hours.

ferrocarril (m.)   railroad

The **fare, Oca, real**ly is not for the porter.
The **railroad** will spend it for metal and mortar.

fiera   wild beast

E**ffie, air a** bed for me at least.
So far, you treat me like some horrid **beast**!

fijo, -a   firm, fixed, secure

A **firm, fixed fee Jo**sé, the lawyer, charged,
By which his bank account was much enlarged.

filo   edge, dividing line, sharp edge

The **fee Lo**renzo charged me for trimming off the hedge
Was more than I expected. It set my teeth on **edge**.

fineza   delicacy, graciousness

Make love to E**ffie? Nay, So**l surely wouldn't.
Her **delicacy** awes him so, he couldn't.

flaco, -a   lean, skinny, thin

The **flock o**'erflowed its fold and scattered.
They looked so **lean** it hardly mattered.

flor (f.)   flower

If **Lor**d Augustus called us to his side,
We came, our native country's **flower** and pride,
Not really caring if we lived or died.

forastero, -a   stranger, foreigner

For a stay romantically grand,
Become a **stranger** is an antique land.

forjar   to fabricate, forge, concoct

Four Harvard men refused **to fabricate**
A tale explaining why they came in late.

foro   bar (legal profession), forum

Four robust young graduates, admitted to the **bar**,
Look around and wonder where the biggest pickings are.

fraude   fraud

The **Frau they** claimed to be a **fraud**
Has up and married Uncle Claude.

fregar   to scrub, scour

If **Ray gar**bled what you said
I'd **scrub** his mouth out till it bled.

freír   to fry

Je**ff, Ray ir**ritates you till you cry,
So you must call the cops and let him **fry**.

frenar   to curb, brake, restrain

Je**ff, rain ar**t on us from all directions.
But **curb** your lectures into bite-sized sections!

frijol (m.)   bean

Care**free, whole**some is the farmer
Who sows this **bean**, as tough as armor.

fruncir   to pucker (nose), furrow (brow)

The rou**gh rune seer**s have touted as prophetic
Puckers the nostrils like a strong emetic.

fuero   jurisdiction, authority

Je**ff, wear o**ld clothes and spread the fiction
You're from some foreign **jurisdiction**.

garbo   gallantry, grace

His **garb, o**'erlaid with gold and lace,
Enhanced his **gallantry** and **grace**.

garra   claw (n.)

My fine ci**gar a** tiger grabbed and ate.
I clipped his **claws** and left him to his fate.

gasto   waste, expenditure

De**gas sto**le no ideas from sinner or from saint.
He knew attempts at rivalry were just a **waste** of paint.

gato   cat

At last I **got o**ld Silas in my grasp.
Quick as a **cat** he wriggled from my clasp.

gelatina   gelatin

All mothers know what **hell a teen a**rouses
When **gelatin** is all the freezer houses.

germen (m.)   germ, cause, origin

The **hair men** brush with so much zest and zeal
Contains the very **germ** of sex appeal.

gesto   gesture

Hess told everyone the tragic truth:
His foolish **gesture** sacrificed his youth.

giro   rotation, trend

He romances girls of every nation
And dates them in monotonous **rotation**.

goce (m.)   enjoyment

Let's **go! Say**, where's the most élite **enjoyment**?
Some other day perhaps we'll seek employment.

golpear   to pound, beat, bump

My **goal: pay Ar**thur for his help,
Then **pound** him till I hear him yelp!

grillo   cricket

I can't a**gree Yo**semite is dead.
It still has **crickets**, though they're less well-bred.

gris   gray

Put goose-**grease** on your sparse **gray** hair in globs,
And end your patient wife's despairing sobs.

grosero, –a   uncouth, coarse

Some **uncouth** men of Montene**gro say ro**mance begins
When couples get together and recount their early sins.

guante (m.)   glove

Aw, **g'wan! Ta**ke back your knightly **glove**.
Why should we duel for a faithless love?

guardar   to keep, guard

The Ja**guar, dar**ling, you can **keep** for free.
Our other cars the judge assigned to me.

guía   guide (m. & f.); guidebook (f.)

Mc**Gee a**ppears to need a **guide**
Through this, his native countryside.

guiso   stew

Those noisy **geese o**ld Hilda can reduce
To hot goose **stew** with lots of good goose juice.

haber   have (aux.)

Ah, bury the hatchet! Be we right or wrong,
We two **have** heard again love's old sweet song.

halagar   to flatter

Allah, guard my love from friends who **flatter** her,
As well as foes who would assault and batter her.

hartar   glut, satiate

Hard-h**eart Ar**thur **gluts** his yen for gold
By turning out the help when they grow old.

hilar   to spin

B**ee, lar**cenous as ever, **spun** a yarn
About some treasure buried in a barn.

hilera   line, row

Coming upon th**e lair a** jaguar cherished,
A **line** of Choctaw Indians almost perished.

hinchar   to swell, bloat

"W**ean Char**les off gin!" his neighbors cry!
"He'll **swell** demand but not supply!"

holgar   to be idle, rest

Wh**ole gar**dens are our care. This handy guide'll
Convince you that we'**ve** not **been idle**.

horca   gallows

For Roman poets, we ad**ore Ca**tullus!
On the very **gallows** he could lull us.

hoz (f.)   ravine

In the **ravine** there live a h**ost** of creatures
Distinguished by some otherworldly features.

hurto   theft, stolen article

Y**OUR toe**, Joe, was wounded in the **theft**.
But by good fortune we have nineteen left.

idear   to devise, plan

The people! S**ee, they are** arising!
It's a plot they'**ve been devising**!

igual   same, equal

YOUR l**eague wall**oped Arthur's league.
He swears he smells a base intrigue!
To you and me it's all the **same**,
For in the end it's just a game.

imán (m.)   magnet

See Mongol hordes sweep on, unmoved by pity,
Drawn by the **magnet** of the Royal City.

impulsar   to impel, drive, urge

The dr**eam pool Ser**geant Sally found
Impelled the squad to stick around.

indio   Indian

Uns**een deo**dorants are those
That leave no markings on your clothes.
Did **Indians** use them? Heaven knows!

influir   to influence

Into my dr**eam flew eer**ie rimes
That **influenced** my life and times.

ingenio   engine

D**ean Henny o**nly watches, filled with pain,
His home-made **engine** rusting in the rain.

insensato, -a   mad, senseless

Scr**een sense Otto** surely never had:
The **mad** galoot just can't play Galahad!

instar   to urge, beseech, insist

D**ean, star**tling news has struck our street.
Please **urge** our PTA to meet!

invierno   winter

We're poor in the extr**eme, Bee. Air no** false pretentions.
In **winter**, beans will have to do for folks who live on pensions!

izquierdo, -a   left (direction)

I saw my n**iece ski, ere tho**se days were over,
From right to **left** across the cliffs of Dover.

jaqueca　　　　headache, migraine

Ha! cake again! It surely looks enticing.
But why use chewing-gum instead of icing?
It's such a **headache** when it comes to slicing!

jaula　　　　jail, cage

Don't start to **howl, A**dele. Just go to **jail**.
Perhaps you'll get a pardon in the mail.

jornada　　　　day's work, journey

You and the long**horn—ah the** wonder of it!
Accomplish each **day's work**—and simply love it!

joya　　　　jewel

—A**hoy, ya** thug, unhand my purse! And give me back my
　　jewel!
—With pleasure, Miss. We sailor boys just love to play the fool!

julio　　　　July

Ma**hooly—oh**, I sadly miss him!
Since last **July** I've longed to kiss him!

lado　　　　side

Oo la **la! though** fame and fortune hide,
I care not, if I have you by my **side**!

lance (m.)　　　　cast, throw

You're still out fishing, **Lon! Say** why at last
You seem afraid to risk another **cast**.

latido　　　　heartbeat, throb

Car**la, tea, though** slightly stimulating,
Will keep your **heartbeat** from accelerating.

latir   to throb, beat

Bel**la, tear**s are lost on Bob.
He has a heart that's ceased **to throb**.

lavar   to wash, launder

Dar**la bor**rows from us, Sundays,
Soap **to wash** her fancy undies.

lazo   trap, loop

Oo la **la! so** many young, provocative Parisians!
They set their **traps** for local lads and try for quick decisions!

leal   loyal

Lay Ollie, ever **loyal**, on his bier.
He'd love this ceremony, were he here!

lectura   reading

Alec, tour a bit (of course you'll do no speeding).
Then try to settle down at home and catch up on your **reading**.

lidiar   to struggle, fight, contend

Lee, the articles of war are signed.
Now I must **struggle** not to change my mind!

liebre (m.)   hare

True, **Lee, Abe rai**sed hell when we drove out last night.
But how could that small **hare** we saw engender such a fright?

lío   fray, struggle

Young **Leo**, captain in our childish **fray**,
When we deserted looked the other way.

lirio   lily

Lee claimed that his business was pure as a **lily**.
But **leery o**ld lawyers soon made him look silly.

liso, -a   smooth, even

The **lea so smooth** appears before us
I'm fain to join the crickets' chorus!

listo, -a   ready, clever, prompt

We sought in vain among the clever planners
At **least o**ld-fashioned **ready** wit and manners.

llover   to rain

Yo**yo, bear** it when it starts **to rain**.
It swells the oh-so-profitable grain.

loro   parrot

Low romantic feeling has this **parrot**.
I offered him a kiss. He chose a carrot.

lozano, -a   vigorous, luxuriant

Car**los, ah! no** rule's so rigorous
It can't be broken if you're **vigorous**!

lucero   bright star

Lou, say romance is moribund or failing.
That doesn't mean our own **bright star** is paling!

lujo   opulence, luxury

Our **Lou ho**pes she'll become (at your expense)
A woman kept in carefree **opulence**.

lumbre (f.)   light (n.)

Il**lume, bra**ve sailors, your great merchant ship.
Its **light** will guide us on our rowboat trip.

macho   robust, male

Ma chose Pa because of what he ain't.
Types more **robust** just make her fight—or faint.

magro, -a   thin, lean

If **Ma gro**ws just a little **thin**ner
We'll let her eat her birthday dinner.

maldecir   to curse

So**me all-day, ser**ious dilemmas
Got roundly **cursed** at my Aunt Emma's.

mancha   spot, blemish, stain

Co**me ON! Cho**p up the goodies in the pot,
But leave the tablecloth without a **spot**!

manchar   to stain, spot

Hoot, **mon! char**coal must not **stain** or **spot**
This kilt, the only decent one I've got.

marchar   to proceed, march

—**Proceed! March Ar**thur to the supervisor.
—I fear he'll leave us both but little wiser!

marido   husband

Ah, **Marie, though** you're omitted from his will,
Your tears beside your **husband**'s grave declare you love him
    still.

marina   fleet

That rude **marine o**ffended Mabel.
She'd sink the **fleet** if she were able.

matiz (m.)   tint, shade, tone

I love **Matisse**'s subtle **tints**.
My walls are crowded with his prints.

mediar   to intervene

May, the article's obscene!
I fear the law will **intervene**!

medir   to measure

May th' eerie tunes that sweetly mix and **measure**
The midnight hours become our two hearts' treasure!

melena   long hair, mane

In sunlit grass **May lay, no**t touched by care,
Till I came by and seized her by the **hair**.

menor   younger, smaller

May, Nora, and their crafty **younger** brother
All make up lies to mystify each other.

mensual   monthly

Dashing **men Sue al**ways sees
Weekly, **monthly**, or when they please.

merienda   picnic, afternoon tea

Mary, end a boring **picnic**.
Just say, "I'm going home. I'm sick, Nick."

mesa   table

May, sop up the brandy you just spilled.
For this my ruined **table** you'll be billed!

mesón (m.)   tavern, inn

May Sonya learn before she meets her date
A **tavern**'s not a place to stay out late.

meter   to set in, put in

May, tear my image from your heart.
Set in its place your love of art.

miembro   member

Believe **me, Em, bro**cades of rich design,
Egyptian scarabs, casks of Tuscan wine
Reward the **members** of our cult divine.

mojar   to wet

Moe hardly ever **wets** the bed
Because the fellow's so well-bred.

molde (m.)   pan

She poured the mix into a **mold**.
Dave ate it ere the **pan** got cold.
You should have heard his mother scold!

moler   to grind

Ai**m, O Lair**d of Glen MacHeath,
To grind your oats but not your teeth!

molino   mill

Ne**mo, lean o**ld workman, in your **mill**
The wheels of yesteryear are turning still.

monje (m.)   monk

A **moan hai**led Brother Peter as the **monks** were saying
    prayers.
Brother John, in ecstasy, had fallen down the stairs!

mora   blackberry

—Is it a prune that caused this stink?
—It's **more a blackberry**, sir, I think.

morder   to bite

Our love is no **more there**. I see but this:
These days I think you'd rather **bite** than kiss.

moreno, -a   dark-haired, dark-complected

More rain! Oh me! I tremble with emotion:
My **dark-haired** lad brought home a lover's potion!

mosca   fly

A lachry**mose ca**reer's ahead for that besotted
Young man who weeps for every moth and **fly** he's swatted.

mostrar   to show

Most rah-rah boys don't last too long,
And **show** small sense of right and wrong.

muerte (f.)   death

Let Willia**m wear ta**me butterflies—yes, even with éclat,
And he'll no doubt be laughed to **death** by folks at Mardi Gras.

nariz (f.)   nose

An**n, a rec**ent poll shows all oppose
Your plans for operations on your **nose**.

nervio   nerve

Ne'er be overtaken on a curve.
Rather, push the gas and drive on **nerve**.

nevar   to snow

Block—**nay, bar**—your door against the blow
And lay in stores before it starts **to snow**.

niebla   fog

Je**nny, Abe lo**st touch in the **fog**.
He was brought home late by the family dog.

nieta   granddaughter

"**Niet," a** word the men we knew as Soviets used to favor,
My **granddaughter** has learned from some old Russian book
     I gave 'er.

nieve (f.)   snow

His injured foot and k**nee Abe ba**thed in **snow**.
His foot is thawed out now but lacks a toe.

nivel (m.)   level

Our bon**ny bell**'s a brazen devil:
It only rings when on the **level**.

nube (f.)   cloud

My **new-ba**ked cookies now received a **cloud**
Of all the powdered sugar Ma allowed.

nudo   knot

There's nothing really **new, though** Jen
Has tied the **knot** with Bob again.

nuera   daughter-in-law

My **daughter-in-law** (I think her name is Sarah)
Led a parade to open a bright **new era**.

nutrir   to nurture, nourish

New tree retreats we built, and from the boughs
We gravely watched the herdsmen **nurture** cows.

obrero   worker, laborer

"**O Brer O**possum," murmured Uncle Remus,
"A clever **worker** Harris was to team us."

odiar   to hate

Joe, the **ar**tist I've been dating,
Knows no art but that of **hating**.

ofrecer   to offer

B**o, fray Sar**ah's bra and costly lace-trimmed pants.
Then **offer** her a cozy seat among the killer ants.

olivo   olive tree

O Lee, bone up on the birds and bees.
Then join me under the **olive trees**.

olor (m.)   stink, odor

—**O Lor**dy, what a frightful **stink**!
—The **odor**'s coming from your sink!

olla   pot

B**oy, ya** positively can't imagine
How many **pots** of stew your gang's been cadgin'!

orar   to pray

I **pray** you may be angels from the skies.
Or are you only humans in disguise?

oreja   ear

O Ray, hop to it! Lend your **ear**.
Some men from Mars are landing here!

ostra   oyster

My h**ost ro**bbed Benedictine cloisters
To serve his guests the finest **oysters**.

otoño   autumn, fall

Oh, tone Yolanda's singing down when Grandmother appears.
You too may long for quiet in the **autumn** of your years.

oveja   sheep

Obey Hawaii's late demand for **sheep**,
So residents can count them ere they sleep.

padecer   to suffer

—Few teachers **suffer** from the Golden Touch.
—The fact is, **Pa, they cer**ebrate too much.

pago   payment

I made your **Pa go** pay your debt,
But this one **payment**'s all you'll get.

paliza   beating, drubbing

—**Pa, Lisa**'s love affair was fleeting.
—Nonetheless, she'll get a **beating**.

palmera   palm tree

True, **Poll MAY ro**b all her loves—the slut!
That's why she lures them to her **palm-tree** hut.

paño   cloth

U**pon Yo**landa's slender form
Even the **cloth** looked lithe and warm.

par   equal, alike

Pa resisted long, but in the sequel
He and his foe agree their teams are **equal**.

pared (f.)   wall

Pa, Ray they find a bit annoying,
Against a **wall** of pride deploying
Those graces that have now grown cloying.

partido   game; departure

Her re**partee, though** hardly tame,
Has added laughter to our **game**.

paseo   stroll, drive; roadway, walk (n.)

Did Grand**pa say o**ld platitudes
While on his **stroll** with other dudes?

pasmar   to amaze, stun, astound

Pa**pa, smar**ter than his children think,
Amazed them when he found the missing link.

pasta   dough, batter, paste

If **Pa sta**rts mixing spices with the **dough**
We'll all be walking in a fiery glow
Like Shadrach, Meshach, and Abednego.

pecar	to sin

You know you must **pay car**fare at the door,
So fork it over. See you **sin** no more.

pegar	to stick

Pay gardeners well, and they will **stick** like glue,
And all your flowers glow like morning dew.

penar	to pine for, long for, suffer

Pro**pane, ar**gon are important gases
That **pine for** recognition by the masses.

peón (m.)	peon, laborer

Pay only what you have to, and grab whate'er you can.
You'll cease to be a **peon** and become a wealthy man.

pequeño	small, little (in size)

"I won't **pay Kane,**" **Yo**landa roundly swore.
"The lock he made's too **small** for my front door."

piadoso, -a	merciful

Pia, though so merciful in seeming,
Enjoys it when she hears her victims screaming.

picante	highly spiced, hot

Chop a **pecan; ta**ke wine that's **highly spiced**,
And mix a fine dessert that's cheaply priced.

pícaro	rogue, knave, rascal

You **rogue**, you s**peak a ro**mantic tongue
That I, too, knew when the world was young.

pico   beak

The market boom has surely reached its **peak**.
O Bird of Fortune, bear me in your **beak**!

pila   heap; baptismal font, basin; battery

Peel a dozen apples on a **heap** of nuts and dates.
Try it, and you'll think you stand before the Pearly Gates.

pisar   to crush, step on

Piece arguments like ours together,
And we can **crush** him with a feather.

piso   floor, story (of a building)

The third-**floor** tenant's rather like a **pea**—
So young, so round, so fresh, so green is she.

plato   dish

The **plot O**'Malley worked so long and hard on
Featured a **dish** of fish with poisoned lard on.
But no one ate it, so he got a pardon.

playa   beach

Ply a trade on bench or **beach**,
Gladly learn and gladly teach,
And grab what money you can reach.

plegar   to fold (clothes, in Spain); pleat

Plague Arthur till he **folds** his underwear
And stows it neatly on his bedside chair.

pleito   wrangle, dispute, lawsuit

My children, stop your **wrangles** and **disputes**,
And learn to **play to**ccatas on your flutes.

plomo   lead (mineral)

Po**p, low mo**rale and too much liquor
Can sink a man like **lead**—but quicker.

poblar   to populate

Bep**po, blar**ney sweetens all your daily conversation.
Oh, that men like you could just re**populate** the nation!

poder (m.)   power

Gesta**po—ther**e's a **power** accurst
That showed a nation at its worst!

poderoso, -a   powerful

Poe, they row so hard, each **powerful** stroke
Sounds like a bombshell to the river folk.

poema (m.)   poem

Poe, aim a poem at Annabel.
She'll reply with a funeral knell.

pollo   chicken

This **poi Yo**landa made with **chicken**; it
Needs more taro though, to thicken it.

porfiar   to persist

Po**p, Orfie ar**gues all night long.
He still **persists**, although he's wrong.

preciar   to price, appraise, value

Pray see Arthurine, and **price**
Her gadget for destroying lice.

presa   prey, booty; dam

I saw Po**p race a** tiger to its **prey**.
The tiger won, and Pop just sulked all day.

presentir   to have a premonition

Du**pré sent eer**ie signals into the tropic night.
I **had a premonition** that the man would die of fright.

presión (f.)   pressure

Pray see only the wealth of good in Gerty.
Sure it's the **pressure** of poverty makes her dirty.

prestar   to be good for, be used for

Don't **press Tar**zan overmuch.
He**'s** only **good for** going Dutch.

presto   soon, quick, ready

Press Tobias to your heart, and **soon**
He's planted there for half the afternoon.

primavera   spring

—Will little **Prima bear a** child next **spring**?
—If I know Prima, not without a ring.

primero, -a   first

In Ca**pri may ro**mance survive
And **first** attachments stay alive!

primor   exquisite beauty, artistry, delicacy

The isle of Ca**pri, more** than wine or wit,
Speaks to my soul of **beauty exquisite**.

proa   bow (of ship), prow

The nautical **pro a**ddressed his fan:
"Lighten the **bow**, sir, if you can."

pródigo, -a   prodigal (n. and adj.)

Each year I see a **pro—the gho**st of Christmas Past.
He comes to warn us **prodigals** this year may be our last.

prorrumpir   to burst into (laughter, tears)

Cries from the **pro room pier**ced the night,
And girls **burst into** tears of fright.

puente (m.)   bridge

Po**p, when Te**cumseh rides across the **bridge**
Be sure you hide the cookies in the fridge.

puerco   pig, pork

Po**p, wear co**rrect attire. And brush your wig.
You can't go bowling looking like a **pig**!

pues   well (interj.)

—Po**p, was**te a nickel twice, you waste a dime.
—**Well**, search for quarters in the sands of time.

puño   fist

The s**poon Yo**landa thrust into my trembling **fist**
Was full of pills provided by the court psychologist.

quiebra   break, fissure

I made a **break** with fris**ky Abra**ham.
He'd proved to be a lion, not a lamb.

¿quién?   who?

The town's **key en**terprise is weaving rugs,
And this it supplements by selling drugs.
Who doubts it's really just a haunt of thugs?

quizá   perhaps, maybe

Perhaps you should tone down your harsh invective.
A low-**key sa**rcasm is more effective!

rabia   rage, fury

Robbie, on fire with invincible **rage,**
Had all his old rivals locked up in a cage.

rabioso, -a   furious, mad, raging

Robbie, oh so fast and **furious,**
Pastes me one if I get curious!

rabo   tail

—Let's **rob o**ld men. They're tired and frail.
—Not now! That cop is on our **tail!**

recado   message, errand

Rake ah! those tender **messages** together,
And see them crumple in the wind and weather.

recelar   to distrust

I can't e**rase a lar**ge suspicion
That you **distrust** my sacred mission.

recogimento   seclusion; house of correction for women

Forgive young D**rake. Oh, he meant o**nly this:
To brighten your **seclusion** with a kiss!

redactar   re-edit, edit, write

Ray, Doc Tarbell surely won't be credited
Unless I have his narrative **re-edited**.

regalo   gift

Craig, aloe leaves will give your mood a lift.
Still better, they're a most impressive **gift**.

regio, -a   regal, royal

Said **Ray (he o**nly hoped his tones were **regal**),
"I rule that your engagement is illegal."

regocijar   to rejoice

Ray, go see Harley. He'll **rejoice**
Despite your coarse, repellent voice.

reinar   to rule, reign

Reign, Arthur, over the realm of the deathless Table Round.
Rule where Lancelot sighed and Kay forever clowned.

reino   kingdom, realm, reign

Your **reign, O** King, has always been serene.
Clearly, your **kingdom** doesn't need a queen.

relato   report, statement; story

By your **report, Ray, lotto** is for kids!
A grownup addict must be on the skids!

reloj (m.)   clock, watch

Rail oh! hard-heartedly at Grandpa's **clock**.
It never will say more than just "tick-tock."

renegar   to deny vehemently, blaspheme, curse

I **do deny** that insect traps and seeds
Can quite replace the **rain a gar**den needs.

reñir   to fight, scold

The tyrant might **reign year**s before he saw
He could not **fight** the people and the law.

reparto   delivery route

Pray part old Henry from his load of loot.
You'll find him on the day's **delivery route**.

resaltar   to stand out, be clear, be evident

—**Ray, Sol tar**nished Grandfather's good name.
—His own **stands out** in chronicles of shame.

restar   to remain, be left over

W**rest Ar**thur's plunder from his clutch.
If aught **remains**, it can't be much.

retrato   picture, portrait

Ray, trot old **pictures** out we took in Rome.
Then we'll be sure our guests will soon go home.

ría   mouth of a river

Ma**rie a**greed to meet me at the **mouth**
Of that great river rolling to the south,
And there pronounce a spell to end our drouth.

rico, -a   rich

Dup**ree co**habits with a local witch,
Who finds her lover raucous, rough—and **rich**.

rienda   rein

Ma**ry, end a** taxing household riot:
Tighten the **reins**, and keep your husband quiet.

rincón (m.)   corner (inside)

St. Patrick's joyous color filled the land.
And so—green hat on head, g**reen cone** in hand—
I huddled in my **corner**, watched the band.

riña   squabble, quarrel

I**rene, yo**n fowl you mean to seize and gobble
Is not the bird to die without a **squabble**.

risco   cliff, crag

A C**ree scho**lastically blest
Dived off a **cliff** with zeal and zest,
But failed the depth-perception test.

robo   robbery, theft

We seized a **robe O**thello might have worn,
But in the **robbery** the hem was torn.

rocío   dew

Jeth**ro, see o**ld Elihu, limping o'er the morning **dew**.
He cannot see, he cannot chew. Is this ahead for me and you?

roncar   to snore, growl

—What makes the old c**rone car**p and croak like that?
—She **snores** a lot; besides, her jokes fall flat!

ropero   closet

Rope Errol, hiding in the **closet**.
Quick in the trash-can him deposit!

rozar   to graze, scuff, scrape

The Skid **Row ser**geant, growing bolder,
Fired his gun and **grazed** my shoulder.

rueda   wheel

When B th**rew A the** timid, tender glance,
The **wheel** of fortune shifted to romance,
And C to Z was all love's ancient dance.

ruego   supplication, entreaty, plea

On thei**r way go** disenfranchised nations,
Some with threats and some with **supplications**.

ruso, –a   Russian

I **rue so** nights I dated that rude **Russian**.
Out of his mouth such flattery kept gushin'!

saco   loot, bag, sack

Sock old Chico in the snoot!
He's the one who lost our **loot**!

sacro, –a   sacred

The **sock Ro**selle laboriously knitted
For this her **sacred** image, never fitted.

sala   family room, living room

Solomon sat in a sate of gloom in a gold-and-ivory palace.
Better my humble **family room** in a three-room flat with Alice.

salida   start, departure

—**Sol, eithe**r you or I must now depart.
—Well, here's your hat. You'd better make a **start**.

salir   to go forth, go out

El**sa, lyr**ic lines as sweet as yours
Go forth and touch the world, for art endures.

salpicar   to sprinkle, spatter, splash

Sol, peek ardently at Beth. She's **sprinkling**
A lotion on to keep her skin from wrinkling.

saltar   to leap, jump

—Take care, **Sol, tar**pon is a feisty fish.
—He'll do no **leaping** in a baking dish!

sañudo, -a   vindictive, cruel

She count**s on you, though** well aware
You're too **vindictive** to be fair.

sapo   toad

Sop old Benji's mess up. Tell that **toad**,
"Go home and dirty up your own abode."

sartén (f.)   frying pan

The chop**s are tain**ted since my Pa began
To store tobacco in the **frying pan**!

sazón (f.)   right time, seasoning, flavor

El**sa, Son**ya only tried by reasoning
To show us the **right time** to add the **seasoning**.

segundo, -a   second (adj.)

Say, goon, don't try that silly trick again.
A **second** goof will land you in the pen!

selva   jungle

It's hard to **sell ba**nanas in the **jungle**,
And bringing beans to Boston's but a bungle!

sellar   to stamp, seal

Say yards of silk are shipped away:
They're lost if not **stamped** "U.S.A."

sello   stamp

The neighbors **say Yo**landa dealt in **stamps**.
She faked so many that her hands got cramps.

seno   breast

So you deny my fond request?
Well, **say no** more. I might have guessed
You have no pity in your **breast**.

sentido   sense

Sen-**sen tea, though** bought at small expense,
Is priceless, for it rouses every **sense**.

silla   chair

I **see ya** sitting in my favorite **chair**,
And yet ya wonder why I stand and glare.

sobar   to pet, fondle

Mel's **so bar**barous he thinks
A man can't **pet** while mixing drinks!

someter   to propose

So, may Terry now **propose**
A plan that only Terry knows?

soneto   sonnet

So Nate owes plenty for Anne's new bonnets?
Just let him pay with a dozen **sonnets**.

sonrisa   grin, smile

Matt**'s own Risa** wears a sickly **grin**
As his familiar anecdotes begin.

súbito   suddenly

I counseled **Sue, "Be to**tally oblivious
To Bernard's glance so **suddenly** lascivious!"

suelo   floor, ground

Take care, Le**s. Weigh low** price against high quality,
And build sound **floors** to bear our high society.

sumar   to summarize, add, sum up

Sue marked the final page and **summarized**:
"To fall in love is often ill-advised."

sumo, -a   highest, supreme

Dear **Sue, mo**nastic rules are here in force.
We brothers lead the **highest** life, of course.

superar   to surpass

Super-arguments like yours
Surpass the spiels of guided tours.

tallo   stalk, stem

Tie Yolanda to a bamboo **stalk**.
Soon or late we're sure to make her talk.

tejer   to knit, spin, weave

Sure-**Stay Hair**-Do's make you sit and sit.
So come prepared to gossip, doze, or **knit**.

telón (m.)   curtain (theater)

Your fish **tale on**ly bored the group. That's certain.
They groaned and stamped till I rang down the **curtain**.

temor (m.)   fear, dread

Tame ordinary birds and make them talk.
No **fear** that people will not stand and gawk!

terco, -a   steadfast, stubborn

Her sorrows **tear Co**rinne apart.
She hides them in her **steadfast** heart.

tesoro   treasure

S**tay sore, o**ld comrade, shun me if you will.
The **treasure** of our past will haunt you still.

testigo   proof; witness

Test Igor next. If she should goof
We'll have the killer and the **proof**!

tez (f.)   complexion

I have little **tas**te for such florid **complexions**,
But cultivate Jim for his social connections.

tibio, -a   tepid, lukewarm

Will **tea be o**ver by half-past six?
Such **tepid** stuff is short on kicks.

tiempo   time

My Aun**tie Em, Po**dunk's new mayor,
Says too much **time** is spent in prayer.

tijera(s)   shears, scissors

That mus**ty hay ro**ts slowly upon our humble bed.
Let's cut the curtains up with **shears** and sleep on them instead.

tiniebla   dark, darkness

Teeny Abe lamented in the park
He's not allowed to play there after **dark**.

tino   good sense, good judgment

—**Tea no** longer do I find relaxing.
—**Good sense** will tell you cocoa's much less taxing.

tinte (m.)   tinge, dye, tint

I saw the **teen ta**ke on a **tinge** of blue
On learning whom her Pa got married to.

tiro   shot, throw (n.)

Please **tee Roe**'s ball. These days he cannot bend.
But he'll be calling **shots** up to the end.

tocino   bacon, salt pork

The boarders, Ot**to, see no** beef or **bacon**,
So tell the cook she'll have to set the cake on.

topar   to bump (into), run (into)

S**tow par**t of our loot in your bra and pants,
And try not **to bump** into maiden aunts.

topo   mole, gopher

Nemo's **toe po**litely wiggling
Set a watchful **mole** to giggling.

torcer   to twist

The thief **tore Sar**ah from her bed.
She **twisted** free and knocked him dead.

toro   bull

Tow romantic milk cows hither.
The **bulls** will put them in a dither.

tosco, –a   rough, coarse

Coma**tose Co**retta slumped.
Of course her paramour was stumped.
On the **rough** floor the girl he dumped,
Then pried the window up and jumped.

trabajo   work

If you, Jeane**tte, rob—ah!—ho**tels and banks,
For all your **work** a jail will be your thanks!

trastornar   to disturb, upset

Bar**t, Ross tore Nar**vik all apart
Because a marvel gripped his heart:
Disturbing yet ethereal flame,
Aurora Borealis came.

tribuna   tribune

That pal**try boon A**dolphus asked for once
The **tribune** granted to some other dunce.

tropel (m.)   rush, bustle; mob

Cas**tro pel**ted us for hours
With cartridges concealed in flowers.
At last we stabilized our powers,
And in a **rush** the field was ours.

tropezar   to stumble

Ki**t, rope a ser**geant like a steer.
But do not **stumble** on your gear.

trueno   thunder

That **roué know**s very well
He's started on the road to hell.
Sometimes he hears a voice of **thunder**
That roars at him "You're going under!"
He whispers, "Lord, just one more blunder!"

tupir   to clog, block, cram, fill, obstruct

Mike's urge **to peer** into the Ladies Room
Clogged all his thoughts and brought about his doom.

último, -a   last (adj.)

—Just drink the water clear and c**ool. Tea mo**stly costs
    too much!
—My friend, this is the **last** time you'll get by with going
    Dutch.

untar   to daub, smear, spread

S**oon Tar**zan will come swinging on the breeze,
Daubing his private mark on all the trees.

usar   to wear, use, employ

Aren't **you sor**ry that you **wore** my pants?
I figured your intention in advance.
That's why you've got a pocketful of ants.

valioso, -a   powerful, influential, valuable

Bali, oh so powerful are your charms
They draw me to you like encircling arms.
(I want to split your landscapes into farms.)

vano, -a   vain, useless

Bah! no woman here is so neurotic
She'd make a **vain** attempt to seem erotic.

vara   wand, rod, stick

Bar a lightning bolt or other hitch,
This **wand** will conjure up my favorite witch.

vela (1)   watch (n.); candle

We'll **bale a** ton of cotton, on the **watch**
That no intruder tries to grab a swatch.

vela (2)   sail (n.)

—Les, my **bail a**mounts to over fifty thousand smackers.
—So set your **sail** for foreign lands and find some heavy
    backers!

velar   to veil, blur, fog; keep watch

His uncle did at last **bail Ar**thur out,
But still the case **is veiled** in clouds of doubt.

venda   blindfold, bandage

Ben dots every *t* and crosses every *i*.
I guess he wears a **blindfold** and it makes him see awry.

vender   to sell

I saw **Ben dare** to barter, knowing well
What deadly stuff he came to buy and **sell**.

ventero   innkeeper

Innkeeper Reu**ben, terro**rized by thugs,
Buried his gold in Oriental rugs.

verdor (m.)   greenness, verdure

—I can't **bear Dor**ca's childish **greenness**!
—It's better than her mother's meanness!

verso   verse

That **bear, so** hunger-bitten and so lean,
Reminds me somehow of my Aunt Irene.
So here's a **verse** to all that's crass and mean.

verter   to tip (over), pour, spill

The she-**bear, ter**rified, **tipped over** chairs
And made a frantic exit down the stairs.

vía (f.)   road, route

Be a good companion on the **road**,
And travel with a greeting, not a goad.

viña   vineyard

If O'Dell by chance has seen ya
Invade his **vineyard**: he will **bean ya**.

viso   sign, hint, indication

Pa, what makes you **be so** saturnine?
I'll try to please you if you'll give some **sign**.

vuelo   flight

I've heard Bo**b wail o**ver **flights** he missed
By stopping for drinks that he couldn't resist.

viveza   liveliness

He can **be base. A** maiden in distress
Might fall for his beguiling **liveliness**.

ya   already

Over **yo**nder stands a pretty lady
Whose fame's **already** getting pretty shady.

zorro   rascal; fox

Don't get **sore, o**ld **rascal**, I just giggled
Because last time you laughed your molars jiggled.

FINAL EXAM

Each of the 40 jingles below contains the sounds of a Spanish word that you have learned from this book. The jingles themselves you have not seen before. They are constructed just like those in the text. Find and underscore the consecutive syllables that approximate the sound of the Spanish word.

When you have finished the test, turn to page 70 and check your answers. If your answers are all correct, you can congratulate yourself on a not inconsiderable achievement.

1. May Nora and her **younger** friends
    Enjoy their luck before it ends!

2. Lon, say why you made your **cast**
    Here where the current runs so fast!

3. Lay Oliver in state upon his bed:
    Another **loyal** follower is dead.

4. Dashing men Sue always sees.
    I think she charges **monthly** fees.

5. Do, Sergeant, **wear** your Sunday uniform
    The night you sneak into the women's dorm.

6. A beau no self-respecting young woman wants to keep
   Is one who reeks of **fertilizer** even in his sleep.

7. I swear by yonder mountain top
   We'll get **there** somehow ere we flop.

8. Bo no doubt forgot to phone us
   To say he'd just OK'd our **bonus**.

9. John taste-tested all the wine
   Before he'd let us start to dine.

10. Ah, Sol, tow icebergs from the Balt—
    Ic for our next marine **assault**.

11. Ray, go see Harley's jars of home-made honey.
    We **rejoice** to see it's not too runny.

12. Hi, you thar, come **help** your dad!
    He first fell down and then got mad!

13. Bah! stop arguing and go to bed.
    With a sincere "Goodnight," **enough** is said.

14. Eric, ah! Bokhara rugs,
    If they escape the local thugs,
    From **end** to end are chewed by bugs!

15. —Why do they keep old Herman on the **team**?
    —They want to help him feed his self-esteem.

16. Free holy men to live in caves.
    (The lowly **bean** will feed the slaves.)

17. He's hero to the kids of all the nations
    For wonderful gyrations and **rotations**.

18. Emma, wreathe O'Malley's grave with blooms
    Like those you've left on all your **husband**s' tombs.

19. Oh, **gild** the lily, paint the rose,
    But back-door art we must oppose.
    So put it where the garbage goes
    Because it, too, offends the nose!

20. That play Tobias wrote brought on a **wrangle**.
    He had to go to court to solve the tangle!

21. At my behest O'Dell explained to Ruth
    Her vulgar **gestures** marked her as uncouth.

22. **Well**, Pop, waste no words on Uncle Jim.
    Blows are the only way to deal with HIM.

23. A spree Ma Bear objected strongly to
    Led me last **spring**, dear Goldilocks, to you.

24. How can the children bear terror like this?
    They **pour** out their hearts to me, die on a kiss.

25. Our car got lost, with all its hungry **load**.
    Bo just sat still and penned a classic ode.

26. Blah, though pretty, trudging by my **side**,
    My sweetheart knows she'll never be a bride.

27. Lark, O herald of the jocund spring,
    You **catch** my heart when you begin to sing!

28. Peter, on his nightly bender,
    Chanced to dent Roberta's fender.
    Within the law, he says he'll send 'er
    A message rather tough than tender.

29. The fracas Art observed while gopher-**hunting**
    Was just some pigs companionably grunting.

30. Ella, tea—though sweet—is only hot.
    Speed up my **heartbeat**, frankly, it does not.

31. The geese o'ertook me ere they knew
    I meant to put them in a **stew**.

32. A bonny belt and sword adorn that devil.
    His manner makes you sure he's on the **level**.

33. You oaf! Race Sarah to her father's coffers!
    She'll take you, since no other prospect **offers**!

34. —O Ray, hard times have hit me. —Friend, I fear
    To pleas for cash I cannot lend an **ear**.

35. **Perhaps** our Corky, sorry that she had blown her top,
    Resolved she wouldn't down a pill or drink another drop.

36. Her cats own Risa, since she took them in.
    She won their trust by her compelling **grin**.

37. The tutor Sarah had that day selected
    Twisted her mind, and made her feel rejected.

38. My friend an extra? Bah! José's a star!
    He'll find you **work**, if only at the bar.

39. Ah, go stow all your implements away.
   It's too much trouble for an **August** day!

40. Ma, roast a duck. Then add some **rice**
   And garnish with a tasty spice.
   You'll find you've whipped up something nice.

ANSWERS FOR FINAL EXAM

1. **May Nor**a
2. **Lon, say**
3. **Lay Ol**iver
4. **men Sue al**ways
5. D**o, Ser**geant
6. **A beau no**
7. by **yo**nder
8. **Bo no**
9. J**ohn tas**te-tested
10. **Ah, Sol, tow**
11. **Ray, go see Har**ley's
12. H**i, you thar**
13. **Bah! stop**
14. Eri**c, ah! Bo**khara
15. th**ey keep o**ld
16. **Free holy**
17. **hero**
18. Em**ma, wreathe O**'Malley's
19. back-**door ar**t
20. **play To**bias
21. be**hest O**'Dell
22. Po**p, was**te
23. s**pree Ma Bear o**bjected
24. **bear ter**ror
25. **car got**
26. Bla**h, though**
27. Lar**k, O her**ald
28. **dent Ro**berta's
29. fra**cas Ar**t
30. Ell**a, tea—though**
31. **geese o**'ertook
32. bon**ny belt**
33. **oaf! Race Sar**ah
34. **O Ray, har**d
35. Cor**ky, so**rry
36. cats **own Risa**
37. tu**tor Sar**ah
38. ex**tra? Bah! Jos**é's
39. **Ah, go stow**
40. M**a, roas**t

GLOSSARY

English	*Spanish*
abridge	cifrar
achieve	conseguir
activate	actuar
actress	actriz
actuate	actuar
add	sumar
afternoon tea	merienda
aid (n.)	ayuda
alike	par
already	ya
amaze	pasmar
ample	amplio
anchor (v.)	aferrar
anguish	congoja
annoyance	disgusto
annual	anual
appraise	preciar
appreciate	apreciar
approve	aprobar
approve of	aprobar
April	abril
architect	arquitecto
argue	alegar
art	arte
artistry	primor

English	*Spanish*
assault	asalto
assist	ayudar
astound	pasmar
atmosphere	ambiente
attack (v.)	acometer (1)
attempt (as a crime)	atentar
August	agosto
authority	fuero
autumn	otoño
avoid	evitar
bacon	tocino
bag	saco
bale	fardo
ball	bola
bandage	venda
bank note	billete
banner	bandera
banquet	convite
baptismal font	pila
bar (legal profession)	foro
barbershop	barbería
barley	cebada
barrier	barrera
basin	pila
batter	pasta
battery	pila
be acquainted with	conocer
be clear	constar (2), resaltar
be evident	constar (2), resaltar
be good for	prestar
be idle	holgar
be in need of	carecer
be left over	restar
be still	enmudecer

English	Spanish
be used for	prestar
beach	playa
beak	pico
bean	frijol
beat	golpear, latir
beating	paliza
become silent	enmudecer
beer	cerveza
before (place)	ante, delante (de)
before (time)	antes (de)
belie	desmentir
bell	campana
bend (v.)	encorvar
beseech	instar
besiege	cercar
bite (n.)	bocado
bite (v.)	morder
blackberry	mora
blaspheme	renegar
blemish	mancha
blindfold	venda
bloat	hinchar
block (v.)	tupir
blur (v.)	velar
bond	bono (1); eslabón
bonus	bono (2)
booty	presa
bore (v.)	aburrir
bored	aburrido
boring	aburrido
bow (of ship)	proa
brake	frenar
break (n.)	quiebra
breakfast	desayuno
breast	seno

English / *Spanish* headers at top.

English	*Spanish*
bridge	puente
bright star	lucero
brio	brío
build	construir
bull	toro
bump (v.)	golpear
bump (into)	topar
bundle	bulto, fardo
burden	carga
burst into	prorrumpir
(laughter, tears)	
bustle	bulla, tropel
buttock (of animal)	anca
cabbage	col
cage	jaula
calm (v.)	aplacar
candle	vela (1)
canopy	dosel
carpet	alfombra
carriage driver	cochero
cast	lance
cat	gato
catch	coger
cause	germen
cease	cesar
center	entraña
chain	cadena
chair	silla
chalice	cáliz
change	cambio
chat	charlar
chatter	charlar
check (v.)	comprobar
cherish	abrigar

English	Spanish
chicken	pollo
choir	coro
chorus	coro
cipher (v.)	cifrar
clatter	bulla
claw (n.)	garra
clear (v.)	despejar
clerk	empleado
clever	listo
cliff	risco
clock	reloj
clog (v.)	tupir
closet	ropero
cloth	paño
cloud	nube
coarse	grosero, tosco
code	código
collect	coger
colonist	colono
comet	cometa
complexion	tez
conceal	esconder
concoct	forjar
confirm	confirmar
consist	constar (1)
contend	lidiar
cool	enfriar
core	entraña
corner (inside)	rincón
corner (street)	esquina
corner store	bodega
cottonwood	álamo
crack (v.)	crujir
crackle	crujir
crag	risco

English	*Spanish*
cram	tupir
creak	crujir
cricket	grillo
crime	crimen
crow (n.)	cuervo
cruel	sañudo
crush	aplastar, pisar
cup	cáliz
curb (v.)	frenar
curse (v.)	maldecir, renegar
curtain (theater)	telón
curve (v.)	encorvar
dais	dosel
dam	presa
damage (v.)	dañar
dance (n.)	baile
dark	tiniebla
dark-complected	moreno
dark-haired	moreno
darkness	tiniebla
daub	untar
daughter-in-law	nuera
day's work	jornada
death	muerte
deceit	engaño
deflect	desviar
delicacy	fineza, primor
deliver	entregar
delivery route	reparto
demolish	derribar
deny vehemently	renegar
departure	partido, salida
despise	despreciar

English	Spanish
destroy	desbaratar
detach	despegar
devise	idear
dew	rocío
dig	cavar
dine	cenar
dinner party	convite
dish	plato
display	alarde
displeasure	disgusto
disprove	desmentir
dispute (n.)	pleito
dispute (v.)	alegar
distrust (v.)	recelar
disturb	desbaratar, trastornar
divert	desviar
dividing line	filo
doormat	estera
dough	pasta
dower	dote
dowry	dote
drawing	dibujo
dread	temor
drink a toast	brindar
drive (n.)	paseo
drive (v.)	impulsar
drubbing	paliza
dwarf	enano
dye	tinte
each	cada
ear	oreja
edge	filo
edit	redactar

English	Spanish
English	*Spanish*
elegance	donaire
elegant	apuesto
employ	usar
employee	empleado
encircle	cercar
end	cabo, extremo
endow	dotar
engage	contratar
engine	ingenio
enjoyment	goce
enough!	¡basta!
entanglement	enredo
enthusiastic vigor	brío
entrails	entraña
entreaty	ruego
environment	ambiente
envy	envidia
equal	igual, par
erect (v.)	erguir
errand	recado
etching	dibujo
even (adj.)	liso
even (adv.)	aún
evil chance	azar
examination	examen
excavate	cavar
excel	aventajar
except	excepto
excess	(en) demasía
exile (v.)	extrañar
expenditure	gasto
exquisite beauty	primor
extract	extraer
extreme	extremo
eyebrow	ceja

English	Spanish
English	*Spanish*
fabricate	forjar
fair (n.)	feria
fall	otoño
family room	sala
fan	abanico
far away	allá
fear	temor
fence	barrera
fence in	cercar
fertilizer	abono
fight	lidiar, reñir
fill	tupir
fill to the brim	colmar
firm (adj.)	fijo
firm (n.)	empresa (1)
first	primero
fissure	quiebra
fist	puño
fixed	fijo
flag	bandera
flatten	aplastar
flatter	halagar
flavor	sazón
fleet	marina
flight	vuelo
floor	piso, suelo
flower	flor
fly	mosca
fog (n.)	niebla
fog (v.)	velar
fold (clothes, in Spain)	plegar
fondle	sobar
foreigner	forastero
forge (v.)	forjar
forum	foro

English	*Spanish*
fox	zorro
fraud	fraude
fray	lío
from	desde
front (in . . . of)	delante (de)
fry	freír
frying pan	sartén
fulfill	colmar
furious	rabioso
furrow (brow)	fruncir
fury	rabia
gallantry	garbo
gallows	horca
game	partido
gelatin	gelatina
germ	germen
gesture	gesto
gift	regalo
gild	dorar
gladden	regocijar
glove	guante
glut	hartar
go forth	salir
go out	salir
goddess	diosa
good judgment	tino
good sense	tino
gopher	topo
grace	garbo
graciousness	fineza
granddaughter	nieta
gray	gris
gray hair	canas
graze	rozar

English	*Spanish*
greenness	verdor
grief	congoja
grin	sonrisa
grind	moler
grip (v.)	aferrar
ground	suelo
growl (v.)	roncar
guard (v.)	guardar
guide (m. & f.)	guía
guidebook (m.)	guía
hand over	entregar
handsome	apuesto
harbor (v.)	abrigar
hare	liebre
hate (v.)	odiar
have (aux.)	haber
have a premonition	presentir
have supper	cenar
hazard	azar
headache	jaqueca
heap	pila
heartbeat	latido
help (n.)	ayuda
help (v.)	ayudar
hide	esconder
highest	sumo
highly spiced	picante
hint	viso
hire	contratar
hold (v.)	aferrar
horn	cuerno
hot	picante
house of correction for women	recogimento

English	*Spanish*
hunt	cazar
hurt	dañar
husband	marido
impel	impulsar
impute	achacar
increase (v.)	acrecentar
Indian	indio
indication	viso
influence (v.)	influir
influential	valioso
inn	mesón
innkeeper	ventero
insist	instar
insulate	aislar
intercept	atajar
intervene	mediar
isolate	aislar
jail	jaula
jealous	celoso
jealousy	envidia
jewel	joya
journey	jornada
jug	cántaro
July	julio
jump (v.)	saltar
jungle	selva
jurisdiction	fuero
keep	guardar
keep watch	velar
kingdom	reino
kite	cometa
knave	pícaro

English	*Spanish*
knit	tejer
knot	nudo
laborer	obrero, peón
lack	carecer
ladder	escalera
landlord	dueño
lash (v.)	azotar
last (adj.)	último
last night	anoche
launder	lavar
lawsuit	pleito
lead (mineral)	plomo
lean	flaco, magro
leap (v.)	saltar
left (direction)	izquierdo
level	nivel
light (n.)	lumbre
lily	lirio
line	hilera
lineage	estirpe
link	eslabón
lithe	esbelto
little (in size)	pequeño
liveliness	viveza
living room	sala
load	carga
lodge (v.)	alojar
long for	ansiar, penar
long hair	melena
longing	anhelo
loop	lazo
loose (v.)	despegar
loot	saco
loyal	leal

English	*Spanish*
luggage	equipaje
lukewarm	tibio
luster	brillo
luxuriant	lozano
luxury	lujo
mad	insensato; rabioso
magnet	imán
male	macho
mane	melena
march (v.)	marchar
marry	casar(se)
martial	bélico
maybe	quizá
measure	medir
meet (for the first time)	conocer
meeting	encuentro
member	miembro
merciful	piadoso
message	recado
meticulousness	esmero
migraine	jaqueca
mill	molino
miss (v.)	extrañar
mob	tropel
mole	topo
monk	monje
monthly	mensual
moor (v.)	amarrar
mouth of a river	ría
mouthful	bocado
nail (v.)	clavar
natural gift	dote
nerve	nervio

English	*Spanish*
noise	bulla
nose	nariz
nourish	nutrir
nurture	nutrir
obstruct	tupir
obtain	conseguir
odor	olor
offer (v.)	ofrecer
olive tree	olivo
opulence	lujo
origin	germen
ostentation	alarde
ought to	deber (1)
overthrow	derribar
overwhelm	agobiar, arrollar, colmar
owe	deber (2)
owner	dueño
oyster	ostra
pain (v.)	doler
palm tree	palmera
pan	molde
parrot	loro
paste	pasta
payment	pago
peon	peón
perhaps	quizá
persist	porfiar
pet (v.)	sobar
picnic	merienda
picture	retrato
pig	puerco
pillow	almohada
pine for	penar

English	*Spanish*
pitcher	cántaro
placate	aplacar
plan (v.)	idear
plea (n.)	ruego
pleat (v.)	plegar
plow (v.)	arar
poem	poema
poplar	álamo
populate	poblar
pork	puerco
portrait	retrato
pot	olla
pound (v.)	golpear
pour	verter
power	poder
powerful	poderoso, valioso
practice (v.)	ensayar
pray	orar
pressure	presión
prey	presa
price (v.)	preciar
proceed	marchar
prodigal (n. and adj.)	pródigo
prompt	listo
proof	testigo
propose	someter
protection	amparo
provide	dotar
prow	proa
pucker (nose)	fruncir
pull out	extraer
purse	bolsa
put in	meter
put the blame on	achacar

English	*Spanish*
quarrel	riña
quick	presto
rage	rabia
raging	rabioso
railroad	ferrocarril
rain (v.)	llover
rascal	pícaro, zorro
raven	cuervo
ravine	hoz
re–edit	redactar
reading	lectura
ready	listo, presto
realm	reino
red–hot coal	brasa
refuge	amparo
regal	regio
rehearse	ensayar
reign (n.)	reino
reign (v.)	reinar
rein	rienda
rejoice	regocijar
remain	restar
remove obstacles from	despejar
report	relato
rest (v.)	holgar
restrain	atajar, frenar
retard	atrasar
rice	arroz
rich	rico
right (direction)	derecho
right time	sazón
right–hand	derecho
road	vía

English	*Spanish*
roadway	paseo
robbery	robo
robust	macho
rod	vara
rogue	pícaro
rotation	giro
rough	tosco
route	vía
row	hilera
royal	regio
rug	alfombra
rule	reinar
rump	anca
run (into)	topar
run over	arrollar
rush	tropel
Russian	ruso
rustle	crujir
sack	saco
sackcloth	brea
sacred	sacro
sail (n.)	vela (2)
salad	ensalada
salt pork	tocino
same	igual
sand	arena
satiate	hartar
saturate	empapar
savings	ahorro
scatter	esparcir
scene	escena
scissors	tijera(s)
scold	reñir
scorn (v.)	despreciar

English	_Spanish_
scour	fregar
scrape (v.)	rozar
scrub	fregar
scuff	rozar
sculpture	escultura
seal (v.)	sellar
seasoning	sazón
seclusion	recogimento
second (adj.)	segundo
secure	fijo
seize	apoderar(se), coger
sell	vender
sense	sentido
senseless	insensato
set back (clock)	atrasar
set in	meter
set up straight	erguir
shade	matiz
sharp edge	filo
shave (v.)	afeitar
shears	tijera(s)
sheep	oveja
shelter (n.)	amparo
shelter (v.)	abrigar
shift	cambio
shine	brillo
shirt	camisa
short	corto
shot	tiro
show	mostrar
shun	evitar
side	lado
sign	viso
sin (v.)	pecar
skillful	diestro

English	*Spanish*
skinny	flaco
skirt	falda
small	pequeño
smaller	menor
smear	untar
smile	sonrisa
smooth	liso
snake	culebra
snore (v.)	roncar
snow (n.)	nieve
snow (v.)	nevar
soak	empapar
somebody	alguien
someone	alguien
sonnet	soneto
soon	presto
space	espacio
spatter	salpicar
sphere	bola
spill	verter
spin	hilar, tejer
splash	salpicar
spoil	dañar
spot (n.)	mancha
spot (v.)	manchar
spread	esparcir, untar
spring	primavera
sprinkle	salpicar
squabble (n.)	riña
stain (n.)	mancha
stain (v.)	manchar
stair	escalera
stalk (n.)	tallo
stamp (n.)	sello
stamp (v.)	sellar

English	*Spanish*
stand out	resaltar
star	astro
start	salida
statement	relato
steadfast	terco
stem (n.)	tallo
step on	pisar
stew	guiso
stick (n.)	vara
stick (v.)	pegar
still	aún
stink (n.)	olor
stock	estirpe
stolen article	hurto
stop	cesar
storeroom	bodega
story	relato
story (of a building)	piso
stranger	forastero
stroll (n.)	paseo
struggle (n.)	lío
struggle (v.)	lidiar
stubborn	terco
student	alumno
stumble	tropezar
stun	pasmar
stupendous	estupendo
stupid	estúpido
suddenly	súbito
suffer	padecer, penar
sum up	sumar
summarize	sumar
supplication	ruego
supreme	sumo
surpass	aventajar, superar

English	*Spanish*
suspicious	celoso
svelte	esbelto
sweet	dulce
swell	hinchar
table	mesa
tail	rabo
take possession of	apoderar(se)
tangle (n.)	enredo
tar	brea
tavern	mesón
team	equipo
tepid	tibio
test	examen
theft	hurto, robo
there	allá
thin	flaco, magro
thrift	ahorro
throb (n.)	latido
throb (v.)	latir
throw (n.)	lance, tiro
thunder	trueno
ticket	boleto
ticket (in Spain)	billete
tie (n.)	eslabón
tie (v.)	amarrar
time	tiempo
tinge	tinte
tint (m.)	matiz, tinte
tip (over)	verter
toad	sapo
tone	matiz
too	demasiado
too much	demasiado

English	*Spanish*
trap	lazo
treasure	tesoro
trend	giro
tribune	tribuna
trick (n.)	engaño
twist	torcer
uncouth	grosero
undertake	acometer (2)
undertaking	empresa (2)
unfold	desplegar
unfurl	desplegar
upset	desbaratar, trastornar
urge	impulsar, instar
use	usar
useless	vano
vain	vano
valuable	valioso
value (v.)	preciar
vase	cáliz
veil (v.)	velar
verdure	verdor
verify	comprobar
verse	verso
vigorous	lozano
vindictive	sañudo
vineyard	viña
voucher	bono
waist	cintura
waistline	cintura
walk (n.)	paseo
wall	pared

English	*Spanish*
wand	vara
warlike	bélico
wash (v.)	lavar
waste	gasto
watch (n.)	reloj; vela (1)
wear	usar
weave	tejer
wed	casar(se)
weigh down	agobiar
well (interj.)	pues
wet (v.)	mojar
wheel	rueda
whim	antojo
whip (v.)	azotar
who?	¿quién?
wide	amplio
wild beast	fiera
wine cellar	bodega
winter	invierno
wit	donaire
within	dentro (de)
witness	testigo
work	trabajo
worker	obrero
wrangle	pleito
write	redactar
yawn (n.)	bostezo
yet	aún
younger	menor